# Barbarians

by the same author

# Barbarians

by
DOUGLAS DUNN

FABER AND FABER
London and Boston

First published in 1979
by Faber and Faber Limited
3 Queen Square London WC1
Printed in Great Britain by
Latimer Trend & Company Ltd Plymouth

British Library Cataloguing in Publication Data

Dunn, Douglas
  Barbarians.
  I. Title
  821'.9'14      PR6054.U54B/
  ISBN 0-571-11316-8

# Contents

# III

## Acknowledgements

Some of the poems in this book first appeared in *Encounter*; *Fortnight*; *Gallimaufry*; *Honest Ulsterman*; *Lines Review*; *London Magazine*; *New Edinburgh Review*; *New Review*; *Poetry Book Society Supplement, 1974*; *Poetry Review*; *Thames Poetry*; *Vole*; and some were broadcast on BBC Radio Scotland and BBC Radio 3.

The Author thanks the Arts Council of Great Britain for a grant received in 1977.

'He was bored, but nevertheless he slowly grew further and further away from the hardship and simplicity of the workers, from his childhood environment. He somehow learned how to behave, as they say. Without realizing it, he cut himself off from his own people. . . . He thought he was merely bored, but secretly he was flattered at being included. Some forces drew him towards the bourgeoisie; other forces sought to retard his transition.'

'The truth of life was on the side of the men who returned to their poor houses, on the side of the men who had not "made good".'

Paul Nizan, *Antoine Bloyé*

# I

## Barbarian Pastorals

# The Come-on

' . . . the guardian, the king's son, who kept watch over the gates
of the garden in which I wanted to live.'
                                        Albert Camus

To have watched the soul of my people
    Fingered by the callous
Enlivens the bitter ooze from my grudge.
    Mere seepage from 'background'
Takes over, blacking out what intellect
    Was nursed by school or book
Or had accrued by questioning the world.
    Enchanting, beloved texts
Searched in for a generous mandate for
    Believing who I am,
What I have lived and felt, might just as well
    Not exist when the vile
Come on with their 'coals in the bath' stories
    Or mock at your accent.
Even now I am an embarrassment
    To myself, my candour.
Listen now to the 'professional classes'
    Renewing claims to 'rights',
Possession of land, ownership of work,
    Decency of 'standards'.
In the bleep-bleep of versicles, leisure-novels,
    Black traffic of Oxbridge—
Books and bicycles, the bile of success—
    Men dressed in prunella
Utter credentials and their culture rules us,
    A culture of connivance,
Of 'authority', arts of bland recoveries.
    Where, then, is 'poetry'?
Brothers, they say that we have no culture.
    We are of the wrong world,

13

Our level is the popular, the media,
   The sensational columns,
Unless we enter through a narrow gate
   In a wall they have built
To join them in the 'disinterested tradition'
   Of tea, of couplets dipped
In sherry and the decanted, portentous remark.
   Therefore, we'll deafen them
With the dull staccato of our typewriters.
   But do not misbehave—
Threats and thrashings won't work: we're outnumbered.
   Drink ale if you must still,
But learn to tell one good wine from another—
   Our honesty is cunning.
We will beat them with decorum, with manners,
   As sly as language is.
Take tea with the king's son at the seminars—
   He won't know what's happening.
Carry your learning as does the mimic his face.
   Know one knife from another.
You will lose heart: don't show it. Be patient;
   And sit on that high wall
In its obstacle glass chips, its barbed wire,
   Watching the gardeners.
One day we will leap down, into the garden,
   And open the gate—*wide, wide.*
We too shall be kings' sons and guardians,
   And then there will be no wall:
Our grudges will look quaint and terrible.

# In the Grounds
*Yorkshire, 1975*

Barbarians in a garden, softness does
Approve of who we are as it does those
Who when we speak proclaim us barbarous
And say we have no business with the rose.

Gently the grass waves, and its green applauds
The justice, not of progress, but of growth.
We walk as people on the paths of gods
And in our minds we harmonize them both.

Disclosures of these grounds—a river view,
Two Irish wolfhounds watching on a lawn;
A spinster with her sewing stares at you,
And begs you leave her pretty world alone.

More books than prejudice in our young minds . . .
We could not harm her, would not, would prefer
A noise less military and more kind
Than our boots make across her wide *parterre*.

We are intransigent, at odds with them.
They see our rabble-dreams as new contempt
For England's art of house and leaf. Condemn
Our clumsiness—you do not know, how, unkempt

And coarse, we hurt a truth with truth, still true
To who we are: barbarians, whose chins
Drool with ale-stinking hair, whose horses chew
Turf owned by watching, frightened mandarins,

Their surly nephews lounging at each gate,
Afraid we'll steal their family's treasured things,
Then hawk them—pictures, furniture and plate—
Round the encampments of our saddle-kings.


## Here be Dragons
Pomponius Mela, *Chorographia*


In Africa, Pomponius Mela wrote,
Are tribes whose bodies stop beneath the throat.
His readers might not marvel much at that
Headless and monstrous proletariat
For Mela says that faces on their chests
Had all the usual features and, unless
Pomponius lied, I can suppose their art,
Doubtlessly oral, came straight from the heart.

There, too, in Africa, were troglodytes
Who housed themselves in the eternal night.
This Mela proffers civilized distaste.
He says of these non-citizens of waste
And downward tunnelled tenements, they dined
On serpents they discovered as they mined.
If they had raised their tenements through sky,
What lunch would fowl-fed Mela specify?

Mela records a tribe that cursed the sun
At dusk and dawn. These people of No-One
Possessed no names and did not dream. Dreamless
Without nomenclature, did Mela bless
That dreamless people who knew more than he
Could ever know of their reality,

Cursing the sun, cursing at dusk and dawn,
For reasons Romans couldn't lay their fingers on?

These then were wonders Mela thought he saw
In lives reported as hair, skin and claw.
That flattered Rome, to keep its *regnum* sure—
The home of shave and soap and manicure.
One story's left, the one that Mela tells
That's their revenge—the one about the well.
Arriving there thirsty and out of breath,
Romans might drink, then laugh themselves to death.


## Gardeners

*England, Loamshire, 1789*
*A gardener speaks, in the grounds of a great house, to his Lordship*

Gardens, gardens, and we are gardeners . . .
Razored hedgerow, flowers, those planted trees
Whose avenues conduct a greater ease
Of shadow to your own and ladies' skins
And tilt this Nature to magnificence
And natural delight. But pardon us,
My Lord, if we reluctantly admit
Our horticulture not the whole of it,
Forgetting, that for you, this elegance
Is not our work, but your far tidier Sense.

Out of humiliation comes that sweet
Humility that does no good. We know
Our coarser artistries will make things grow.
Others design the craftsmanship we fashion
To please your topographical possession.

A small humiliation—Yes, we eat,
Our crops and passions tucked out of the view
Across a shire, the name of which is you,
Where every native creature runs upon
Hills, moors and meadows which your named eyes own.

Our eyes are nameless, generally turned
Towards the earth our fingers sift all day—
Your day, your earth, your eyes, wearing away
Not earth, eyes, days, but scouring, forcing down
What lives in us and which you cannot own.
One of us heard the earth cry out. It spurned
His hands. It threw stones in his face. We found
That man, my Lord, and he was mad. We bound
His hands together and we heard him say—
'Not me! Not me who cries!' We took away

That man—remember, Lord?—and then we turned,
Hearing your steward order us return,
His oaths, and how you treated us with scorn.
They call this grudge. Let me hear you admit
That in the country that's but half of it.
Townsmen will wonder, when your house was burned,
We did not burn your gardens and undo
What likes of us did for the likes of you;
We did not raze this garden that we made,
Although we hanged you somewhere in its shade.

# The Student
## Of Renfrewshire, 1820

For our Mechanics' Literary Club
I study Tacitus. It takes all night
At this rough table which I always scrub
Before I sit at it, by candlelight,
Spreading my books on it. I think respect
Must work like love in any intellect.
> *Difficult Latin sticks in my throat*
> *And the scarecrow wears my coat.*

What put me up to it, this partnership
Of lexicon and text, these five books thieved,
These two books borrowed, handed down, this grip
Of mind on mind, this work? Am I deceived?
Is literature a life proved much too good
To have its place in our coarse neighbourhood?
> *Difficult Latin sticks in my throat*
> *And the scarecrow wears my coat.*

In Paisley when they read the Riot Act
We faced the horsemen of the 10th Hussars.
Men's bones were broken, angry heads were cracked—
Provosts, sheriffs, guns and iron bars.
We thrashed the poet William Motherwell,
That depute-sheriff and the law's law-minstrel.
> *Difficult Latin sticks in my throat*
> *And the scarecrow wears my coat.*

Between us and our lives were bayonets.
They shone like water. We were crooked with thirst,
That hot dry bubbling when your whole life sweats.

'If you want life', they said, 'you must die first.'
Thus in a drought of fear Republic died
On Cocklesloan, George Street and Causeyside.
> *Difficult Latin sticks in my throat*
> *And the scarecrow wears my coat.*

Beneath our banners I was marching for
My scholarship of barley, secret work
On which authority must slam its door
As Rome on Goth, Byzantium on Turk.
I'm left to guess their books, which precious line,
Eluding me, is never to be mine.
> *Difficult Latin sticks in my throat*
> *And the scarecrow wears my coat.*

*Frost, poverty, rare, rare, the rapid rain . . .*
What good can come of study, I must have.
I read it once, then read it twice again.
Fox, whittrick, dog, my horse, my new-born calf—
Let me recite my life, my animals and clay,
My candlelight, my fuddled melody.
> *Difficult Latin sticks in my throat*
> *And the scarecrow wears my coat.*

Such hard work urges me to turn each line
As firmly as I plough a furrow straight,
By doing so make this work clandestine,
Mix its affections with both love and hate.
So, Tacitus, old friend, though not to me,
Allow me master your authority.
> *Difficult Latin sticks in my throat*
> *And the scarecrow wears my coat.*

# An Artist Waiting in a Country House

An artist waited in a country house
Set in a park, before a lake, and old.
He waited for a lady who had asked
To speak with him, for she had bought his works
And wished to make enquiries of his meaning
And his methods. From where he sat, he saw
The lady walking with her husband, who,
In riding boots, seemed something less than eager
To meet this person who was waiting in
A room that past munificence had warmed.
It seemed to be the finish of an argument
In which both he, the artist, and the lady,
Were subjects of a fanciful connivance
Or were accused of what they'd not intended.
He watched her husband kiss her on the cheek
And leave for somewhere else. He waited, sure
That her arrival was a matter of
A moment. He waited, waited, seated on
A sofa and the minutes passed, unlived,
More cinematic than anonymous.
He felt he'd walked into a private story.
Perhaps no one remembered where he was ?
The room was one of fifty. They'd been built
When palaces were populous, and arts
Of masque and figure graced decisive eyes,
An architecture of success and wealth
In far, disreputable trades, or in
The purse of government, the secret gold
Of families. All artists know their pasts,
Those flung purses, when it was proper to
Ignore what now it is improper to
Ignore. Though does that matter much? He'd come

Because that lady asked, although he'd sensed
An obsoletion in the visit, an
Overdone propriety of interest
He felt was serious and entertaining,
Its charm undoubtedly, and why he'd come.
*Let it happen*, he wished aloud, waiting.
The minutes passed, unlived, and still. The room
Was furniture, an art, a heaven to
The fingers of the artisans who'd made it
While on the walls hung noted pictures by
Those other artists who had waited there,
The old originals. His gaze went out
Into the patterned cloth that shaped a chair
Into a fantasy of foliage,
And with it went the function of his eyes.
His eyes were where they should be, on his head;
And yet they were displaced. His mind thinks straight
Most of the time. Some days, to help him work,
Or justify, he bends his mind—just so—
On finding oppositions, those opposed
To what he knows but does not understand
Of what he does, believing it is art.
That day, he stared, so hard that sounds became
Factors of that patterned cloth, so deep
In colour where his gaze had taken him,
And not the slams of doors, or heels on floors,
Or voices raised as if forgetful of
Whatever urgency had made them raised;
Or children running on the crispy leaves;
Or that unskilful pianist playing tunes
Which his or her mistakes made beautiful.
Upon that chair, that lovely patterned cloth,
His gaze lay down. His mind and gaze were sly
And glozed by whispering an entrance to
The chair's amoral world, then went inside

To walk among unlikely foliage
Sensing delight, at one with the delights
Of a serenity, themselves serene, set free.
And loosed to pure inquiry they became
Spectators of release, spectators of
Themselves, himself. And it is terrible
To watch your own eyes watching you, intent
On clarity, from sockets that will twitch
To subtle judgments. By being gone from him,
He felt regret, and holding up his hand
To touch his eye, he touched its gift, a swim
Of body-water one had left behind,
A moistness on his eye, almost a drop.
Invisible fractures in everything.
An error in a pianist's luck. Barking.
The rattle of a dog-cart's wheels. Delights.

He looked behind him. The door had not opened.
When would it open? He was not sure.
He wanted it to open, and to smile,
On standing up, his hand stretched out
To shake the lady's hand and thank her for
Her acquisition of his several pictures.
Then he was sure. It would be always shut.
He would be there, sitting, waiting, always,
The woman always kissed upon her cheek,
Her husband turning, moving, to his stables
Or wherever or whatever or whoever
Was in this private story he had entered
Like a reader who was half-asleep, one eye
Reading as the other lived the story.
He waits, although that door will never open,
Unless he opens it, and walks away
And leaves the pictures hanging in the room
Focussed on the sofa where he waited.

The woman, passing there, will stop, her hand
Will almost knock, almost reach the handle,
With the dry reds of the leaves falling
And children running on the dry, bright leaves,
In histories, like timetables, changes
Approximately chronicled as *happened*,
Something wrong in an unlucky autumn.
One moment forever, and his gaze stuck
In the lovely patterned cloth of a chair,
So inadvertent, like his own mischance—
Heels on the wooden floors, doors slamming—
It might not be happening, though it is,
For what is melting on his cheek is proof,
The tear-drops of a melting eye, his gaze,
And round him stare the old originals.


## Rough-cast

Grey, white, or cream, solid before
Rain, wind, rent-rises or the siege
Protracted in the memories
Of 'exiles' or the lost—*walls, walls.*
Their plaster hooks have grazed young skin.
A 'rough exterior' . . . Inside
The clumsy hearts sit, warmed to truth
Or sentiment in the reports
Of sons, nephews or the aged aunt,
In drink, or by attending to
The thing in the corner that speaks,
That shows, that is of pictures but
Is not of better things shut out
By it. Hearts, houses, do not fit

In this sweet place of stuntedness.
Twelve years away and I cannot
Break out. I cannot do it.
If soul and intellect have made
Their own rooms, then they are like these,
With stairs, sinks, bowls, a table, bread,
Mirror and furniture, of light
Crept over them that lately slipped
Over the hills and factories
And out of seas, as well as walls
That in moonlight run like a milk
Of clotted grey. Walls are involved
More than late sun on rowan berries
Or the ears of a hare above grass
Or a docken sprinkling its rusts.
Or pages noted when rain drummed
On afternoons, and a chill thought
Made walls open, made doors open
To acres sung through by laverock,
Told me the lie that everything
In this world could be touched and loved . . .
Epiphanies, mistakes, the lie.
Who knows this too and runs away
From it, also a poison-dwarf,
To the palavered refinements of
Arts called 'impartial' and the 'fame'
That is a smear on honesty?
Better to root here among ferns
Close by home with those others who
Are devising their justice, sunk
In their holes in the ground somewhere.

# Empires

All the dead Imperia . . . They have gone
Taking their atlases and grand pianos.
They could not leave geography alone.
They conquered with the thistle and the rose.
To our forefathers it was right to raise
Their pretty flag at every foreign dawn
Then lower it at sunset in a haze
Of bugle-brass. They interfered with place,
Time, people, lives, and so to bed. They died
When it died. It had died before. It died
Before they did. They did not know it. Race,
Power, Trade, Fleet, a hundred regiments,
Postponed that final reckoning with pride,
Which was expensive. Counting up the cost
We plunder morals from the power they lost.
They ruined us. They conquered continents.
We filled their uniforms. We cruised the seas.
We worked their mines and made their histories.
*You work, we rule*, they said. We worked; they ruled.
They fooled the tenements. All men were fooled.
It still persists. It will be so, always.
Listen. An out-of-work apprentice plays
*God Save the Queen* on an Edwardian flute.
He is, but does not know it, destitute.

# The Wealth

*When he returned to New York in December 1965, he figured his stay would be a brief one, that he'd earn $25,000 if he was lucky, enough to live comfortably in England. Instead, he earned ten times that much. The success—and the terrors that accompanied it—had begun.*

Paul Cowan, on Paul Simon
*Rolling Stone, 1 July, 1976*

If I prove nothing to you, it's my fault.
The planet's round and greedy.
This song-infatuated globe can't handle it,
In love with rip-off and reward.

It is an old perdition to be rich,
An old displeasure to be seen dismayed
With what you wanted, when, having it, it hurts
Or turns against you in the night.

The last day of December '65
I got a letter from your Uncle Sam.
I'd thought of him as one of the good guys,
Stern, dressed in a dollar, but on our side.

By then I was in two minds.
A lot of people were dying, like clichés.
I wasn't even an American.
Gabe read my papers over, then we hit the town.

The Go-Go girls brought New Year in
Dancing on our table—*Snoopy, hang on!*
I didn't lose my mind in drink. I sulked.
The night-club scooped me up and took me home.

I walked to the bus depot in the snow.
January. They took us to Cleveland.

I didn't want to go. Nick said, 'Go. Buy time.'
We walked around, afraid in underpants.

Faced with a form, I opted for the Coastguard,
'And don't let me see any damn fool
Write "coastguard", gentlemen', yelled a sailor.
There were six-foot-six football giants

Who fainted away in the lottery
Of the blood-test. I wouldn't have missed it,
Not for anything. I didn't faint. I felt—
I felt *proud*. And then *I* couldn't pee in the cup.

A doctor said, if he was me, he'd go back
To Scotland. 'Randall Jarrell', I said. '*Huh?*'
The man next in line pushed me, and asked
If I was 'some kinda coward'. 'Yes', I said.

I said I wasn't an American.
You can't say that to a man in blue jockey-shorts
Who'd been insisting on the Marine Corps.
'A medical is close enough', I said.

If that man went to Vietnam, I hope
He didn't die, or kill anyone,
Or help reduce thin children to
An orphanage of ash.

We used to visit in Peninsula, Ohio,
A precious farmhouse on a wooded hill.
I planted corn, walked on an Indian trail,
James Fenimore Cooper for a day.

The poems in my head were facing west
Towards a continental summer.

I won't deny it. The Stars and Stripes
On a blue autumn day is quite something.

But then, so was I, in casuals,
Fit and young, athletic, frivolous—
As if nobody knew me then—one round year married,
My wife in tears at having to go home so soon.

I liked old villages with soldier-statued squares
Where I could stand and feel like Robert Lowell.
Still there, and probably the same,
Each with its radical son and its casualty.

States of long trains and the astounding autumn,
I squeaked before your laws, reduced
To nakedness, my penis in a cup
Refusing Uncle Sam his specimen of me—

My health, portrayed in Akron's
Tax-paid chemicals, *Cutty Sark*,
Upper New York State wine—oh, Liz, *your* wine!—
And food bought in the Kroger Store.

We shipped aboard SS *United States*.
I went home on a name
With nothing like enough
To live on comfortably.

I felt like a Jew, at Hamburg
On a boat bound for America,
A Jew at Hamburg, 1932,
And wept for laws, but not for me, civilian,

Writing poetry, seasick on the North Atlantic,
Reading *Henderson the Rain King*

And *For the Union Dead*.
I wanted it torpedoed, by the British.

But, for you, a terror was beginning . . .
Such is the magnitude of song.
An American critic, writing of
An English poet who thinks himself classical,

Has said of tenderness, it is
'The social face of self-pity'.
If I say, tenderly, I am afraid,
Who do I fear, or what? *Horror*. 'The wealth! The
    wealth!'

America, I admit it. You've beaten me.
I'll end up in a regiment of *foederati*
To be led forever by a minor Belisarius
Against my kin in the forests of Europe.

Our armoured herds are grazing on the map.
And so are theirs. I write this for *détente*,
Which, as ever, should be personal.
One false move then, I'd have no right to speak.

In your culture, I am a barbarian,
But I'm that here, and everywhere,
Lulled by alien rites, lullabyed with remorse
Here on the backstreets of the universe.

**II**

# Elegy for the lost Parish

Dream, ploughman, of what agriculture brings,
Your eggs, your bacon to your greasy plate;
Then listen to the evening's thrush that sings
Exhilarated sadness and the intimate.

Your son's in Canada, growing his wheat
On fields the size of farms, and prosperous
On grain and granary. His world's replete
With life and love and house and happiness.

Dream, ploughman, of the lovely girl who died
So many summers gone, whose face will come
To you, call to you, and be deified
In sunlight on one cut chrysanthemum.

A nod of nettles flutters its green dust
Across small fields where you have mown the hay.
So wipe your brow, as on a scented gust
Your past flies in and will not go away.

Dream, ploughman, of old characters you've known
Who taught you things of scythe and horse and plough;
Of fields prepared, seed rhythmically sown,
Their ways of work that are forgotten now.

Remember, sir, and let them come to you
Out of your eye to mutter requiem,
Praising fidelities, the good of you.
Allow their consolations, cherish them

Into a privacy, as, with hand's slow shake
You reach towards your glass, your hands reach to
Where no one is or can be. Heartbreak,
Heartbreak and loneliness of virtue!

B

# Watches of Grandfathers

They go with corporations
And with fountain pens,
With honour and inscription,
Fastidious longevities
In which are reckoned
The funerals of friends.

Worn in relation to work,
Timetables, opening times,
And counterparts carried by
Despicable referees,
They are neat in the palm of a hand.
Always to be dangled before

Babies in prams, consulted
With flourishes that invite
Benevolent side-glances,
They have a kindness
Which the artistry of time
In its steady circles

Denies, as it measures
Proximity to pensionable age,
Or, from a safe hook
In the corner of a workshop,
Hung there, stare at the bench
As they mutter 'Death, Death'.

They long for the pocket
Of the eldest son, in
The waistcoat he will buy for one,
Who will see his father's eye
Glazed on it, and the age
Of his sons slowly numbered.

## Portrait Photograph, 1915

We too have our place, who were not photographed
So much and then only in multitudes
Rising from holes in the ground to fall into smoke
Or is it newsreel beyond newsreel
But I do not know and I have lost my name
And my face and as for dignity
I never had it in any case, except once,
I think, in the High Street, before we left
For troopships and the farewell pipers,
When it was my turn in the queue
In Anderson's Photographic Arcade and Salon,
In my uniform, and I was not a tall man
Although for a moment I had a sense
Of posterity in the eyes of descendants,
Of my own face in a frame on a small table
Over which her eyes would go, and my sons',
And that I would persist, in day and night,
Fading a little as they say they do.


## Alice

The story of Alice, my aunt who died
Before I ever breathed—only sixteen—
Was made entirely of the colour white.
She's buried somewhere I have never been.
I leant upon a sideboard of sunlight
As my grandmother told us of it.
She told it often and my father tried
To listen. My mother tried. That was for me.

I let that story whiten endlessly.
The faces just couldn't come through.
Too white . . . I think I died that year—I died:
*White cloths on the river-bank, pink meats*
*That blurred again to white; grandfather, dead,*
*Raising a glass like wine-breath to his head;*
*Tufts underneath the laundered picnic sheets,*
*The men in shirt-sleeves and the women kneeling.*
Eating an apple, they could hear me chew.
My ear was smacked. They said I 'wasn't listening'.
There were apples at that picnic, I knew;
The noise that smack made sounded like applause.
I was sure of it as I chewed, as I knew
That, Alice, it was white, it was you
I tore off piece by piece in my slapped jaws.


## The Musician


They've told me MacAuley is gone now
Taking his tool-box and both his fiddles.
They are saying, '*What will we do now?*
*There is no music in this or the next parish.*'

Until a replacement is found there
Not one note will be heard after whist
Unless it is played from a record—
That, even the young say, won't be as good.

They will talk of MacAuley forever there,
Long after their own receipt of pensions,
Of his carpenter's wrist on the fiddle-bow
Stitching like mad through jig-time.

And so I have heard on the telephone
MacAuley is gone now, and both his fiddles
Lie in their cases under the stairs
With the music we never knew he could read.

It is Beethoven and Bach, they tell me,
And a very fat volume, a German tutor,
That cost six shillings before the war,
And its pages, they tell me, are black with notes.

It's your carpenter's wrist they remember
In love with your local tradition.
Your carpenter's fist could not break through
To the public of Bach and Beethoven.

So they've told me MacAuley is gone,
Both his fiddles lie under the stairs now
With music by Bach and Beethoven
Beside six bob's worth of ambition.

Let them open your window frames, open your doors,
Think, as they sit on their mended chairs,
Of you, their musician, and doctor to wood,
That no one has heard what you understood.


## Drowning


Why give the place its name, when it has changed,
Where, in the grasping waters of the Gryfe,
He, his name forgotten now, was drowned?
What is remembered is his little life.

Ask any man of forty-odd or so,
He'd think a bit, as if he had to try
To bring that name back from its tragedy,
Though, struggling with the tide, he saw him die.

One I could ask was wild, swam in the buff
Where Gryfe's clean waters raced the greedy Clyde
Beside that bridge where ladies parked and watched.
To dry himself, he ran the countryside.

Kirk elder now, who shot the sparrows down
With airgun resting on a garden fence,
How fares your soul, handing out the hymnals,
Who in your sin worked wicked innocence?

One I could ask has crossed the Scottish seas.
From Canada, we've heard no news at all.
He took his boots, his two sly winger's feet.
We miss that man as if he'd pinched our ball.

Most stayed at home, or near it, so they drink
On Friday nights or Saturdays and where
Men know each other and suppress remarks
On sagging bellies or receding hair.

One I could ask has fired his life away
With bottle after bottle to his mouth;
Raw liquor in the turpitude of ditches
While blubbering a sermon on his youth.

Ask any man of forty-odd or so
Around that parish by the Clyde's run sweat,
He'll shake his head as if he has forgotten,
Then walk away, and wish he could forget.

Remember, how we ran up to the bank
And, naked, how we screamed and jumped right in?
Those ladies, watching, must have thought we tried
To please them with a courtesy of skin.

That was our time, and after he was drowned.
It did not mean we had forgotten him.
It is a law, to disobey scared parents.
What better pool than his in which to swim?

But watch the changing waters, when the tide
Runs up, its shoulders hunched, with winking eyes,
And with a nip of sea and a dark surface
It steals the calm reflection from the sky.

They worked him free. They packed his clothes around
    him.
They sat him on his bike and wheeled him home.
Too young for swimming then, I was in goal,
When, from our pitch, I saw the dead boys come.

## Glasgow Schoolboys, Running Backwards

High wind . . . They turn their backs to it, and push.
Their crazy strides are chopped in little steps.
And all their lives, like that, they'll have to rush
Forwards in reverse, always holding their caps.

# Red Buses

*'The last Western'*

Galoot and lover, homeward drunks
Through Govan, Linthouse, Renfrew Cross
Have known well the sudden lurch
Of double-deckers to the digestive system.
God help the man who pukes on his seat
Or is tempted to impertinence.
He will have no Requiem
Nor in the Golf Inn will there be sung
Delicate character studies;
No pawky *éloge* in the Wallace Arms
Nor in the crowds of Glasgow be missed
Among umbrellas and young women in
Greatcoats selling *Morning Star*.
For these are the plain facts of the matter:
No longer will singing be tolerated
Nor the mess created by those
Who cannot hold it in, but who
Must forever be incontinent.
From now on are conductresses instructed
To put the boot in at the first signs of
Contraventions of these Orders—
And our women, as you know, are worse than our men,
Whose only function is,
In this business, to take prisoners.
Therefore, you who have lost your hearts
In San Francisco or who sing
Of your mother's eyes, take warning . . .
Already you will have heard how
Sundry gung-ho Yankee submariners
Have found themselves airborne at Bishopton.
They walked around, amazed

In the night of council houses.
One we heard of slept in the garden
Of a distinguished JP, waking
Under a coverlet of leaves and dew
To sing sad songs of Ohio
Or wherever it was he came from.
We will no longer brook misbehaviour,
Not even from presbyterians.
So, revise your youths. Forget
Your indiscretions on the back-seat
And the disasters of carry-outs
In paper-bags not strong enough
For the purpose. From now on you will walk home.
If it drives you crazy to listen to
Softly ticking factories; or if
Under the tenements you feel you are
In a Glencoe of the mind; or if
Cranes, shipyards, sleeping it off
In the sweat of forgotten labour
Are better served in peace than you are;
Or if, by the bonded warehouses,
You see the square root of all distillations;
Or if you have forgotten the road
And get lost forever in the first
Mattress of West-bracken, the first
Gaunt countryside of the West, then that
Is your fault. You will not be alone.

## Ballad of the Two Left Hands

When walking out one morning
   Walking down Clydeside Street
I met a man with two left hands
   Who said he was obsolete.

At noon the work horns sounded through
   The shipyards on Clyde's shore
And told men that the day had come
   When they'd work there no more.

Economy is hand and sweat
   A welder in his mask
A new apprentice pouring tea
   From his father's thermos flask.

And soon these men of several trades
   Stood there on Clydeside Street
Stood staring at each new left hand
   That made them obsolete.

'Beware of men in suits', one said
   'Take it from me, it's true
Their drivel economics'll
   Put two left hands on you.'

All in the afternoon was shut
   When I walked out again
The day had pulled on its black gloves
   And turned its back on men.

I walked the dusk of darkened cranes
   Clyde broke on Clyde's dark shore
And rivets fired where men still work
   Though men work here no more.

High in the night's dark universe
   I saw the promised star
That men I knew raise glasses to
   In an illegal bar.

They toast that city still to come
   Where truth and justice meet
And though they don't know where it is
   It's not on Clydeside Street.

With thumbs stuck on the wrong way round
   In two left-footed shoes
I saw a man search in his heart
   And ask it, 'Are you true?'

That man who sat on Clydeside Street
   Looked up at me and said
'I'll study this, then I'll pick clean
   The insides of my head.'

And moonlight washed the shipyards then
   Each crane was hung with stars
Rinsed in the moonlight we stared up
   Like old astronomers.

Economy is hand and sweat
   And foundrymen and fire
Revise your textbooks, multiply
   Your guilt by your desire.

Such dignity, so many lives,
   Even on Clydeside Street
When mind and heart together ask
   'Why are we obsolete?'

# Warriors

*'O arms that arm, for a child's wars, the child!'*
                                        Randall Jarrell

Though never in the wards of the hospital for
Disabled servicemen at Erskine—First World War—
I saw an old man wheelchaired through its park one night
By an old man who was blind. The candles were alight
On chestnut trees, a lame destroyer on the Clyde
Was being nursed by tugs against the highest tide
Of May to its dismantlement. The wheelchaired man
Was watching, too, telling his friend, that veteran
And blinded one, all that was going on. No shock
Of pride or pity moved me then. Dumbarton Rock
Rose in the dusk, my own Gibraltar. History
Was everywhere as forts and battles, conscripting me.

My mother went to Erskine once with ladies from
Inchinnan Women's Guild. In bed when she came home,
I heard her tell my father how moved she'd been by these
Blinded basketweavers and nimble amputees.
In my imagination, there is a special place
For that night, for that Park, and for the expert face
Of the man in the wheelchair, and his friend who was
    blind.
If that is wrong, or nearly patriotic, I don't mind.
To me it's neither. For they had suffered all that gore
We played at, and made me see that as a guilty war,
A childhood. Neither willingness or wounds would lead
Me to them from the field. In no war would I bleed.

## Lost Gloves

I leave my body in a new blue suit
  With my soul, which is newly destitute.
Rinsed spirit of me, washed for this departure,
  Takes off adroitly to its atmosphere.

And here's that blue glove on a railing's tip
  Where iron, frost and wool make partnership
Of animal and elements and blue—
  Lost little glove, I still remember you.

You do not fit my hand now, nor can I fit
  My world with life; nor my mouth match its spit;
My tongue, my words; my eyes, the things they see.
  My head is upside down in memory.

A child walks to his mother, right hand bare
  And hidden in his coat, then follows her
Inside, his gloved hand on the banister,
  His right hand on his heart, remaining there.

My pulse beats backwards to a street in winter—
  Blue first perceived, that I now disinter
Blue out of blue where life and childhood crossed:
  Five blue wool-fingers waving in the frost.

## Stories

Once, once, O once upon a time—
I wish that's how a poem could begin,
And so begin one. That's how stories should.
The sweet parental voices started so,
Opening a book, *my* book, one given by
An aunt and uncle, inscribed 'for Christmas'.

No story ever did, I think, unless
Its author, sitting down, said, 'O I wish
That *this* is how a story could begin',
And so began, his tongue half in his cheek.
*Once, once, O once upon a time—*
It's real, magnanimous, and true! I wish,

And wish, and so my friends lose patience with
My stories and they say, 'So this piece is
A story of lost gloves, and, yes, I know
I lost *my* gloves, but why this story, *this*,
This *making-up?*' *Once, once, O once upon*
*A time*, before gloves, gauntlets, politics . . .

*Never, never, never, never, never* . . .
That's a *good* line. And there was one which took
My senses to adventure on a day
Of wind and rain . . . 'One more step, Mr Hands,
And I'll blow your brains out!' *Once, once, once, once* . . .
I think the alphabet is tired of life.

'But be contemporary!' they shout, thumping
The table, and 'Yes, Yes', I say, 'I'll buy
That, all or nothing. Just you wait, you'll see.
I'm of the times . . . My pulse is topical,

And I love all the things I'm meant to love,
Am civil and "sincere", one of the boys.'

Ah, that's better. I mean, I mean it *all*.
Yet when I start to write, my pen puts down
*Once, once, O once upon a time . . .*
And that's for nothing and for no one,
Not anyone, not even for a child
Who, at a table by a bowl of fruit,

Sits down to read. It is too personal,
One sorry pass. I'll give away my thought
Of knowing that a life-discarded petal
Fell down, so slowly, when, a child, I read,
And landed on a page and was brushed off.
*Once, once, O once*, that happened so, like that—

Tender descent—and for a moment was
Completed by its image on the polished
Table. I took it in, did not forget.
Then, *am* I good? Was *that* benevolent?
Now, dignity of tables and of books,
What do *you* say? '*There is no answer, friend.*'

III

## Stranger's Grief
*i.m. Robert Lowell*

It's as if I've grown old, sitting like this
In a small park by the Lot in Cahors
Where autumn is arriving through its mist
To surprise my life with its metaphor.

In an *Observer*, four days out of date,
I've read the poet Lowell's dead. . . . New York,
New York, where smoke and whisky concentrate
Their traffic, architecture, art and work.

Across this river which is brown and fast
There is a paddock boys are running round,
Each one determined not to finish last.
Breath from their mouths drags after them like sound.

That's where the summer stops and autumn starts.
A gentle cadence in the wind will sing
Natural elegies, its counterparts
Of human sadness drowned in everything.

Youth's country is impossibly across
A wide river. How anyone can come
From there, and not look back, or feel no loss,
Always amazes me. I call youth *home*;

I'd go back if I could. I don't feel warmed
By death. To die is nothing very grand.
This world is delicate and misinformed.
It's growing old I've failed to understand.

What else can I do, feeling this way, but sit
With my wife and my newspaper, well-fed,

Well-wined, happy together and unfit.
Is it a happiness like this, being dead?

A radio, its non-specific song
Far away in a leafy park . . . I'm full
Of my routine sadness. It can't be wrong
To let these thoughts run free and overrule

Tranquillity, absorbing time and place,
And what I've read, and you and me, each half
Of this one silent couple, face to face,
As still as lovers in a lithograph.

It is like waiting, learning how to die,
Opened to sweetness, neutral as a leaf
Watching leaves falling. Notice how they lie,
How each survivor shares each stranger's grief.

## Night-Devon, Dawn-Devon

It is with fear, with shame also we raise
Embarrassed eyes to placid galaxies
Where science, stars and planets graze
In fields of God-knows-what. Impieties,
Michael, impieties, that flatter nerve
As does this morning dew on naked feet,
A relish of something. We do deserve
Better than this, our metres obsolete
Contraptions with which words might seize
Wingbeat of kingfisher, the breeze
Through which it flew, or a berry that glows
So close upon a girl's cheek they are the same
And metaphors. We take the blame. It goes.
It leaves us faceless, two smiles in a frame.

# On Her Picture Left with Him

On trains to London and the south
    And thus away from me
These words in my enamoured mouth
    Summon the flattery
Of who it is and what I love,
    Distracting me.

Lady, so far outside, and gone,
    Your picture left with me
Is like the world I look upon
    And shows reality
As who it is and why I love,
    Distracting me.

Thus do I gaze on you, and drink
    Your face you left with me,
And speak to you in whispered ink
    With that humility
Which is a lesser spoil of love,
    Distracting me.

Now is the afternoon turned round
    To dusk that darkens me,
And walking on nocturnal ground
    Offers no liberty
From who I am and who I love,
    Distracting me.

# A Late Degree

She stands there holding her valise
Under the timetable for optional seminars,
And is herself a bag, or so they say
In our bullying, cruel vernacular.
She is in the prime of her infidelity
To a man against whom little can be said,
Of whom little can be said with conviction,
For or against or any other way.
At forty, she has gone late to university
Where she has learned enough to say in public,
Of him, 'He does not understand my life.'
And she knows that he, too, is bewildered.
For she will not grow, nor he grow either—
Not out of the literature she reads
In the publications she takes from her valise
And puts on the coffee table, outrageously;
Nor from the dull reports of his office
Which is secure, exhausting and lucrative;
Nor in the denim in which she looks too much
A woman anxious for your first consideration;
Nor in the new suit in which he attempts to bloom;
Nor in the young men who avoid her eyes
At wine-and-cheese parties at the end of term
Though somewhere, in the pedestrian subway
Or by the racks for bicycles, she has thought,
'I, too, am real.' One short-lived, botched affair
Mishandled in a Hall of Residence—
'Do you want coffee first, or afterwards? . . .'—
And in the coach, returning from Shakespeare.
Is it that consolidates her, warms her
To anger at her sinks, to tears by cassettes?
Daily he disregards her education.

54

The door of his car snaps like a terrible jaw.
He has lunches, the typing-pool, dim-witted wives
Of his colleagues, who she always detested,
Preferring her paperbacks, her books of verse.
Daily she enters confusion, wonders at
Small blows directed against her, arrogance
Of those younger directed against her,
Against a woman so intent on her sexuality—
Which is unbearably sad, unworthy of satire,
For there is no vernacular of compassion.


## The Difficulty


From the body of murdered Rosa
Many visitors have come to me here,
Some with winks and sly congratulations,
Some with big eyes and accusations.

This would make better sense if I had been
An activist, and betrayed activity.
But I have betrayed nothing and no one.
No one has suffered because of me.

Some women are commensurate with the Age.
Their passions rise with the ideas
That struggle with our times for what is good.
They are born, not without beauty,

But into mind that matched with femininity
Creates compassion; and not the nerve
Or fury of a petroleuse or shrew,
The names by which they murdered you.

Hypatia, slaughtered by a bigot-mob
For her philosophy and womanhood,
Once raised her skirts before a pupil,
Saying, 'This only is what you want to know.'

Oh Rosa, led into a car by a lieutenant,
Then clubbed by one called Runge, they shot you,
Dumped your body in a mean canal
Hoping, dead, you'd stink like them, alive.

When I heard of this, I heard you say,
Again, that one like me, a poet,
Need not feel ashamed of my passivity,
Nor rush the streets with my revulsion for

Temporal politics and forms of order
Not laid down by the unconscious Gods
Who pulse and giggle in mythologies.
But years went by. I thought I knew my place;

Your murderers found me out in any case.
So, with my luggage, headed west, my desk,
My books, most of my papers left there with
My cat—know, woman, mind, you I adored,

I am dishonoured in my love of you.
Not fellow-travelled ever, no side taken
In all those years since you've been gone—
A minor talent, surely: not bronze, but stone.

And one, who, loving, lived in worlds apart,
With moments of a mystery, with words,
A touch of leaves from childhood on my senses.
To live one's only life inside that moment!

## Transcendence

Fish-smelling bedroom of the gutted heart;
A port built for departures, dockside bars—
Flat town, that's warm and sleazy, here's your art:
A climb on excrement to reach the stars.


## Old Things

Time and removal vans
Scatter dead widows
From their dying children.
It is late, secretly.
It is a late era
In the grey-stilted rain.
And you who pilfer
In shops of second-hand
Among shabby heirlooms,
Accumulating bits
Of blue pottery, a chair,
A vase, a baby-grand,
Consider—now it's late—
What things come up for air
Out of such furniture,
Whose-hands in the polish,
What-lover's-eye upon
Pendants of amethyst,
Whose-name you wear inside
Whose-bangle on your wrist.

# Wedding

Confetti in the gutters,
Half a dozen leaves
That reach here from autumn,
Yearly . . . What point is there
In regretting no shrubbery
Or abundance of green
Hallows this couple, when the car
The groom has worked on for weeks
Takes them down a street
Elated by love and community?
There is one season
For poverty, and delight
Overlaps all things.

# The Return

'Grey skies are just clouds passing over.'
Duke Ellington

The window-cleaner carried
A cloth bag full of change
And it rattled the tariff
Of window-panes.

There are his ladders
Left by the wall.
There is his pail. There is his rag.
But the windows are broken.

Houses are empty
And rusting aerials sing
A congress of metal and wind
And indifferent sparrows.

Gushed soot on the hearths,
Heaps of plaster, split timbers,
Sodden newsprint and wreckage of armchairs
Litter ripped living-rooms.

I dreamt of perfection.
My dreams have come home
To die here and cling to
My anarchy of convictions.

If only there were no such troubles.
My politics vanished
To the end of the street
Where beauty and pollution meet

In natural ecstasy,
A hint of trees
By the abandoned railway
And a red sunset.

And this is the house I owned,
My two sufficient rooms.
There is no trace of me
As I look for signs

Of 'little jobs' I did about the house,
Domestic, studious, and in love,
Three things, or so I'm told,
I should have fought against.